LANDMARK HAWAII
Sites and Sights of the Islands

1

A catamaran takes in the scenery in the waters off Hawaii's most famous landmark, Diamond Head.

LANDMARK HAWAII
Sites and Sights of the Islands

HAWAII VISITORS BUREAU MARKER

Photographed by Douglas Peebles

Mutual Publishing

CONTENTS

ISBN 1-56647-332-2 Oahu
      1-56647-334-9 Maui
      1-56647-333-0 Kauai
      1-56647-335-7 Big Island

Mutual Publishing
1215 Center Street, Suite 210
Honolulu, Hawaii 96816
tel. (808) 732-1709   fax. (808) 734-4094
e-mail: mutual@lava.net
www.mutualpublishing.com

First Printing, October 1986
Second Printing, March 1989
Third Printing, October 1991
Fourth Printing, October 1995
Fifth Printing, August 1999
Sixth Printing, July 2000
Seventh Printing, October 2001

Printed in Korea

FOREWORD

Landmark Hawaii represents over a dozen years of photographing in Hawaii. The photographs could easily be called Hawaii's "greatest photographic hits," as they are the images of the landmarks and scenic attractions most often seen and enjoyed by visitors to the islands and most often requested for use in magazines and advertisements. Many of them have found their way on to postcards sent either to comfort the shivering folks back home on the mainland or to make them envious with sights of lush green tropical foliage, verdant mountains, and sparkling beaches.

I have made repeated visits to many of these places to capture their dramatic changes from day to day, or even at different times of the day. The photographs presented here are my favorite representations highlighting the array of color that in my opinion best captures the ambience of the scene.

All of the photos in this book were shot with a 35mm single lens reflex camera using either Kodachrome 64 or Fuji 50 film. For color negatives I recommend Kodacolor 100. When I go out shooting, I usually pack in my camera bag two camera bodies, a small tripod, and the following lenses:

16mm, 20mm, 28mm, 35mm, and an 80–200 zoom. A polarizer is an important accessory for shooting in Hawaii, because it helps bring out the deep blues and many shades of green of the sky, the ocean and the mountains.

All of this may be too much equipment for most people to carry around when having fun and sightseeing. Do the best with what you have. Hawaii is an incredible place to photograph. Enjoy it.

Douglas Peebles

The quiet, glassy
waters of Kaneohe Bay
are a popular sailing
and fishing destination
in Hawaii.

INTRODUCTION

Can a single photograph of a famous landmark serve as an international language anywhere that you may travel in the four corners of the earth?

It can if you're from Hawaii and if the photograph is of Diamond Head. No matter where you are, you can always communicate that you're from Hawaii by showing a photograph of this instantly recognizable landmark . . . and then pointing to yourself.

Diamond Head is only one of Hawaii's many familiar landmarks, though. Through the years, millions of visitors to our islands have returned home with countless numbers of photos and slides of Hawaii's scenic attractions to show their neighbors, family, and friends.

Waikiki Beach is one of the most-photographed places. Then there is Iao Needle on Maui, Hanalei Bay on Kauai, and the black sand beaches of the Big Island.

Or who can resist snapping a photo of one of those giant waves that come roaring on the beach during the winter months on Oahu's North Shore? Or committing to film one of Molokai's most-beloved landmarks, Father Damien's church at Kalaupapa, where he tended and ministered the leper colony.

Sunsets over the beaches and mountains are also favorites. In fact, if at dusk you look up at hotel lanais in Waikiki or Kaanapali, it's almost impossible to count the numerous camera flashes.

Rainbows continue to fascinate tourists and locals alike, and Hawaii certainly has its share of these marvelous ephemeral delights. They make a perfectly beautiful mountain or valley scene an even more breathtaking sight to behold.

Throughout each island of Hawaii you will find many picturesque landmarks that beg you to take their picture. Some of them are landmarks made by nature like the towering volcanoes that formed the islands. Some are man-made like Iolani Palace, home to Hawaii's monarchs. And some, geographers would argue, are really not true landmarks but only scenic landscapes pleasing to the eye.

All of these sights, wherever you find them in Hawaii, have one thing in common, and that's the sense of wonder they instill in you, the deep appreciation of the beauty of the islands that makes these images remain in your heart and mind forever. In the pages that follow you are able to enjoy all of them thanks to the camera skills of one of Hawaii's finest scenic photographers.

OAHU

The island of Oahu is Hawaii's most popular island. Most visitors begin their vacation on Oahu, and with good reason. Oahu is home to Honolulu, Waikiki Beach, Diamond Head, and many other popular tourist destinations.

Landmarks abound on Oahu, with some of the most familiar images of the Hawaiian Islands found throughout the beaches, mountains, and city.

In addition to Diamond Head, you'll find both Punchbowl Crater and Koko Head Crater on the south side of the island as well as Hanauma Bay, a sparkling jewel of a bay, where you can actually hand feed brightly colored tropical fish while you snorkel.

Sheer cliffs, 1,186 feet high and cut by thousands of years of erosion, characterize the Nuuanu Pali on the island's windward, or eastern side.

Oahu is also famed for its deep, amphitheatre-headed valleys, like Manoa Valley, often topped with fluffs of white clouds. Inside these valleys you'll find a tropical wonderland of orchids and ferns clustered around a waterfall.

With all these dramatic landforms and the cosmopolitan city of Honolulu, it's no wonder that Oahu continues to be one of the world's favorite vacation spots.

OPPOSITE PAGE:
A romantic night in Waikiki, with the moon just beginning to put on a spectacular show.

ABOVE: The sun creates a golden glow as it bids "Aloha" to Aina Haina on Oahu.

RIGHT: A tiny island of coconut palms attracts explorers in the Hilton Hawaiian Village lagoon. In the foreground is the Ala Wai Yacht Harbor.

BELOW: The Royal Hawaiian Hotel sits like a glittering pink jewel surrounded by spectacular high-rise hotels.

10

OPPOSITE PAGE: The glittering night lights of Waikiki create one of the world's most spectacular nighttime scenes.

BELOW: What would Waikiki Beach be without a beachboy surfing atop an incoming wave?

An awe-inspiring
panoramic photograph
shows all of Hanauma
Bay, an underwater
refuge for marine life
on Oahu.

Mt. Olomana and Kailua
as seen from the Pali
Lookout at dawn.
Olomana is one of the
highest peaks on Oahu.

LEFT: One of Oahu's most famous landmarks, the Nuuanu Pali Lookout, looking down the Koolau Mountains toward Kaneohe.

BELOW: Two Hawaiian sailing canoes anchored at Kualoa Beach. Chinaman's Hat is in the background.

19

OPPOSITE PAGE:
Byodo-In Temple at the
Valley of the Temples in
Kaneohe is a replica of a
900-year-old Japanese
temple.

LEFT: A Hobie catamaran
race at Kailua Beach Park
is just about to spring
to life.

ABOVE: Rabbit Island
glows in the sunlight
off Makapuu Beach.

21

OPPOSITE PAGE: "The Pageant of the Long Canoes" at the Polynesian Cultural Center in Laie is one of the many colorful events celebrating Polynesian life.

BELOW: Windsurfers race off of Diamond Head, where almost constant offshore winds create the perfect windsurfing conditions.

BELOW: Surfing at the famous Sunset Beach on the North Shore of Oahu.

RIGHT: In the summer, Waimea Bay is calm, perfect for swimming and diving. In the winter, it has some of the largest waves and strongest currents on Oahu.

24

World-champion surfer
Shaun Thomson surfs
"off the wall" next to
the Pipeline on the
North Shore.

BELOW: A pineapple-upside-down cake in the making basks in the sun on Oahu's North Shore.

RIGHT: Twenty-five-foot waves crash onto the rocks at Kaena Point, accessible only by four-wheel-drive vehicles.

BELOW: Aloha Tower as seen from Sand Island. Built in 1921, it was the tallest building in Hawaii until 1963.

RIGHT: Hawaii Hall at Bishop Museum. Founded in 1889 in memory of Princess Bernice Pauahi Bishop, the museum showcases Hawaiian and Polynesian art and artifacts.

Iolani Palace in downtown Honolulu, built in 1882 by King David Kalakaua, is the only royal palace in the United States.

BELOW: King Kameha-
meha Statue, across the
street from the Iolani
Palace, is covered
with plumeria leis to
celebrate the start of the
Kamehameha Day
parade on June 11.

RIGHT: More than
28,000 soldiers are laid
to rest at the National
Memorial Cemetery of
the Pacific inside
Punchbowl Crater.

36

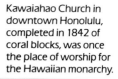

Kawaiahao Church in downtown Honolulu, completed in 1842 of coral blocks, was once the place of worship for the Hawaiian monarchy.

BELOW: The Mission Houses, built from 1821 to 1828, were the first wooden dwellings in the Hawaiian Islands, and were home to the American Congregationalist ministers.

OPPOSITE PAGE: Sunrise at Lanikai Beach on Windward Oahu. The Moku Manus, also known as the Twin Islands, are in the background.

MAUI

"The Valley Isle" of Maui is swiftly becoming one of the world's premier playgrounds by offering the perfect blend of climate and scenery in a relaxed "country/ cosmopolitan" atmosphere.

One of the most popular visitor sites on the island is the town of Lahaina, notable for its missionary heritage, as the former capital of Hawaii, and as the center for the whaling industry in the 1800s.

Kaanapali Beach, Wailea and Kapalua all offer an array of some of the most luxurious resort hotels, restaurants, and boutiques to be found anywhere in the world.

For those who prefer a slower pace, there's Hana, a quiet ranch town at the extreme eastern end of Maui. Situated at the end of a scenic twisting road, Hana offers the ultimate in idyllic isolation.

Maui's most impressive natural landform rises high above the island in unparalleled splendor: Haleakala. It's a dormant volcano on the eastern side, measuring 10,023 feet above sea level. Its crater is a massive nineteen miles wide and is large enough to hold all of Manhattan Island.

Other landmarks to see on Maui are the world's largest banyan tree in Lahaina, the 1,200-foot-tall mountain pinnacle, Iao Needle, and Molokini Islet.

OPPOSITE PAGE: Lahaina, once a major port for whaleships, is protected by the West Maui mountains.

ABOVE: Sunset at Fleming's Beach. Adjacent to the Kapalua Bay Hotel, Fleming's Beach is one of the most picturesque beaches on Maui.

BELOW: Replica of Diabutsu, the Great Buddha in Kamakura, Japan, at the Jodo Buddhist Mission in Lahaina.

RIGHT: The Iao Needle is a 2,250-foot volcanic cinder cone located in the Iao Valley State Park above the town of Wailuku.

Front Street in historic
Lahaina town still retains
much of the charm of the
old whaling days, when
Lahaina was capital of
the Hawaiian Kingdom.

A panoramic view of Lahaina Harbor. Once the whaling center of the Pacific, it is now known for pleasure boats and fishing.

Kaanapali Beach is home
to some of Hawaii's
finest and most luxurious

LEFT: A sunset cruise begins a spectacular seaward trek from Lahaina Harbor.

BELOW: Divers leap from the black rock at Kaanapali every evening at sunset.

OPPOSITE PAGE: Kapalua Bay Hotel sits majestically against the sheltered bay, surrounded by million-dollar condominiums and an excellent golf course.

BELOW: Molokini, located off Wailea and Kihei, is the remains of a volcanic cinder cone that is a favorite of scuba divers and skin divers alike.

Beachgoers enjoy the
sun and sand at one
of several beaches
fronting the resort
community at Wailea.
West Maui is in the
background.

Orchid farming in the
West Maui Mountains
provides many of the
flowers used for leis,
arrangements, tropical
drinks, and hotel pillows
at night.

OPPOSITE PAGE: It's a long drive up to the summit of Haleakala and it's usually cold and windy, but sunrise at the top is something to behold.

BELOW: Haleakala National Park is a 28,660-acre park with a lunar-like landscape where astronauts have been trained.

BELOW: Hookipa is a world-famous spot for wave riding, the fastest-growing sport in Hawaii.

RIGHT: The start of the women's professional wave-riding competition. At Hookipa.

BELOW: Hamoa Beach is a private sunspot maintained for guests of the Hotel Hana Maui in Hana.

RIGHT: A waterfall drops into the Seven Pools area, which is part of Haleakala National Park. There are seven pools, linked by waterfalls, going up into the hills.

Halfway between Hana town and Seven Pools is the misty, sparkling Wailua Falls.

57

OPPOSITE PAGE: The Hana Road curves on the bluff in the distance. Only fifty-two miles from Kahului, it has 673 curves and over sixty one-lane bridges.

BELOW: Just outside of Hana is one of Maui's few black sand beaches. This one at Waianapanapa is actually made up of tiny black stones.

BELOW: A view of Hana Bay and Town from Lyons Head. Hana was a sugar mill town until the 1940s, and is today known for the Hotel Hana Maui.

OPPOSITE PAGE: Deep ridges in the West Maui mountains are the result of volcanic activity.

MOLOKAI

Molokai is the fifth largest island in the Hawaiian chain, being a slender strip of land only thirty-seven miles long and ten miles wide.
But what it lacks in size it more than makes up for in the warmth of its people. Its nickname is "The Friendly Island."

Kaunakakai is the principal town on Molokai, and its main street consists of quaint, wooden false-front buildings that haven't changed much since the 1930s. The land surrounding the town is mainly agricultural, and development throughout Molokai has been limited, with the result being a delightfully rural flavor.

Kalawao on the isolated north coast was the home of Father Damien De Veuster of Belgium, who arrived in the early 1870s to minister to the leper colony. A popular activity today is a mule ride down the steep, winding cliffs to the quaint town of Kalaupapa.

Halawa Valley is a four-mile-long and half-mile-wide tropical wonderland. At the head of the valley are two waterfalls that feed a stream flowing into the sea.

OPPOSITE PAGE: Kalaupapa Peninsula and the North Shore of Molokai, including the Siloama Congregational Church at the abandoned leprosy settlement of Kalawao.

ABOVE: St. Philomena, Father Damien De Veuster's church in Kalaupapa. Damien served the lepers from 1873 until he died of Hansen's disease in 1889.

BELOW: A popular ride
and tour on Molokai is
the mule ride down the
steep switchback trail to
the Kalaupapa Peninsula.

OPPOSITE PAGE: The
highest sea cliffs in the
world are found on the
north shore of Molokai.

BELOW: Wailua Beach and Wailua Valley, the largest on the island. Mostly abandoned, it is a favorite of hunters and fishermen.

OPPOSITE PAGE: A remote heiau on the eastern slope of Molokai. In the distance is Maui.

LANAI

Lanai is the sixth largest of the Hawaiian Islands, and lies eight miles west of Maui and seven miles south of Molokai. It's a rocky seventeen-mile-long and thirteen-mile-wide island that is primarily used today for pineapple production.

It is, in fact, the "world's largest pineapple plantation," since ninety-eight percent of Lanai is owned by the Dole Company, who is its main employer.

There are only about twenty-five miles of paved roads on Lanai, with the only town being Lanai City. Lanai is not what your travel agent would call "a resort island," but it has a surprising number of hiking trails that are popular with those looking for a wilderness vacation.

One of the unusual areas on Lanai is the "Garden of the Gods," where you'll find oddly shaped boulders and rock formations carved by wind and erosion, along with disfigured lava formations.

OPPOSITE PAGE: Ninety-eight percent of the island of Lanai is owned by Dole Pineapple Company. The fruit is of very high quality and is used fresh, not canned.

ABOVE: Lanai Petroglyphs, known as the Luahiwa Petroglyphs, are found about a mile outside of Lanai City, just above the pineapple fields.

KAUAI

The oldest of the Hawaiian Islands, Kauai, is nicknamed "The Garden Island" because of its abundant rainfall and lush vegetation. The colorful Waimea Canyon is found here, and is often called "The Grand Canyon of the Pacific." The fifteen-mile-long Na Pali coastline, with its sharp high cliffs dropping spectacularly to the ocean below, is another well-known landmark. Along this coast is the beautiful Kalalau Valley, totally isolated and accessible only to hikers and boaters.

Other scenic points of interest are Hanalei Valley and Princeville on the north side of the island and the Wailua River on the east side. Kauai is the only island that has navigable waters. A boat ride upstream on the Wailua River takes you to the Fern Grotto. The wettest spot on earth is also found on Kauai at Mt. Waialeale near the Alakai Swamp, with an average 450 inches of rainfall a year.

Kapaa, on the east coast, has the island's largest population, but Lihue, several miles south of Kapaa, is Kauai's principal town and commercial center, as well as the Kauai County seat.

OPPOSITE PAGE: Hanalei Bay with a Hawaiian canoe and Hanalei Pier in the background. The pier was used in the movie **South Pacific** and was built in 1912.

ABOVE: Waimea Canyon is often called the Grand Canyon of the Pacific. It's over a mile wide, 3,600 feet deep, and is especially colorful near sunset.

BELOW: The Wailua River boat tours go up the river to the Fern Grotto. On the right is the Kamokila Village, a re-created Hawaiian settlement on an old village site.

LOWER LEFT: The famous Fern Grotto is found at the lush area at the end of the Wailua boat cruise. It is a very popular spot for weddings.

BELOW: This double stand of eucalyptus trees on the road to Poipu is known on Kauai as the Tree Tunnel. The trees were planted in 1911 by Walter McBride.

OPPOSITE PAGE: The Spouting Horn blowhole at Poipu is caused by surf surging through a lava tube, resembling a whale's spout.

At the Hanapepe Salt
Flats, salt is gathered
using the same methods
the early Hawaiians used.

At the top of Kokee
State Park looking down
into Kalalau Valley, you
will often see a rainbow,
sometimes even a
double one.

LOWER LEFT: A rare sunny day at the summit of Mt. Waialeale. It's the wettest spot on earth, with an annual rainfall of more than 450 inches a year.

BELOW: According to legend, the Alekoko Fishpond was built for a Kauai prince and princess by the legendary menehunes.

BELOW: The Kilauea Lighthouse was built in 1913 and is now a wildlife sanctuary, especially known for seabirds such as boobies, albatrosses, and frigates.

OPPOSITE PAGE: Princeville on the north shore of Kauai is a popular 11,000-acre resort with an excellent golf course and twenty-one tennis courts.

A panoramic view of Hanalei Valley. The vast wet area on both sides of the river is used for farming taro, which provides the Hawaiian staple food, poi.

BELOW: An aerial view
of Hanalei, with its
cresent-shaped beach
and plantation-style
homes.

LEFT: Recognize that point at the end of the ridge? It was used as Bali Hai in the movie **South Pacific**.

BELOW: The Na Pali Coast, one of the most beautiful spots on earth, as seen from a helicopter.

BELOW: Eons of erosion from rain and surf can be seen on the spectacularly rugged Na Pali Coast.

OPPOSITE PAGE: The remote Kalalau Beach is found at the end of the eleven-mile Na Pali Coast trail, built by the ancient Hawaiians.

HAWAII

The island of Hawaii is not only the youngest of the Hawaiian Islands, it is also the largest, thus its nickname, "The Big Island." It covers over 4,034.2 square miles and comprises almost two-thirds of the state's total land area.

Mauna Kea is the highest point in Hawaii, stretching skyward to 13,796 feet. Mauna Loa, another famous Big Island landmark, is a 13,677-foot active volcano. Kilauea Volcano has also created quite a name for itself with its recent spectacular eruptive phases.

The Big Island's sheer size and varying elevations contribute to the incredibly diverse flora and fauna found on the island. Mauna Loa's windward slopes receive up to 300 inches of rain a year, while some areas of the Kona coast are desert. And yes, you can snow ski in Hawaii, as snow falls every year on the summits of Mauna Loa and Mauna Kea.

Sugar production and cattle ranching are the primary uses for agricultural land. Macadamia nuts, coffee, papaya, and horticultural products are also important island crops.

The Big Island also is a treasure trove of historical and archaeological sites and is the birthplace of Kamehameha the Great, who unified the Hawaiian Islands.

OPPOSITE PAGE: The tranquil Liliuokalani Gardens at Hilo with a reflecting pond adding to the serenity.

ABOVE: Kilauea Volcano springs to life during a spectacular May 1986 eruption.

BELOW: The lush, tropical beauty of Rainbow Falls. Located near Hilo at the Wailuku River State Park, the falls are eighty feet high.

OPPOSITE PAGE: Wailua Falls tumbles through the rich vegetation along the Hamakua coast, surrounded by palm and African tulip trees.

OPPOSITE PAGE:
Hawaii's best-known
black sand beach is
Kaimu at Kalapana, and
is one of the island's
most-photographed
scenic attractions.

BELOW: Kilauea, in
the Big Island's Hawaii
Volcanoes National Park,
is among the most active
volcanoes in the world.

A panoramic view of the Kilauea Caldera, site of many ancient offerings to the volcano goddess Pele. Mauna Loa looms in the distance.

OPPOSITE PAGE: The Puukohola Heiau was built by Kamehameha the Great in 1791 as a temple for his family war god, Kukailimoku.

BELOW: Wooden ki'i images guard the reconstructed temple, Hale-o-Keawe, at the City of Refuge National Park.

The City of Refuge was a sanctuary for Hawaiians who had broken the kapu. If they could reach the city, they would escape punishment for their crimes.

Near the King Kameha-
meha Hotel is located
the restored Ahuena
Heiau, and the mortuary
platform where the
bones of Kamehameha
the Great were prepared
for burial.

LEFT: Kona, the home of Kamehameha, was once capital of the Hawaiian Kingdom. It's now a world-renown spot for game fishing.

BELOW: The tiny St. Peter's Catholic Church in Kona sits in an idyllic setting beside the sea.

BELOW: Sunset at Kona with a cruise ship at the horizon's edge.

RIGHT: An aerial view of Kailua-Kona.

104

Hulihee Palace in Kona was built out of coral and lava in 1838, and was used as a summer palace by many of the Hawaiian royalty.

BELOW: Mauna Loa as seen from the slopes of Mauna Kea. Mauna Loa rises to 13,677 feet and is often topped with snow in the winter.

OPPOSITE PAGE: Haupuna Beach Park, one of the Big Island's favorite recreational areas on the Kohala Coast, offers excellent swimming and snorkeling.

BELOW: The original Kamehameha statue, lost at sea and recovered after a replacement was installed at Honolulu, now stands at Hawi in Kohala.

LOWER RIGHT: The Kohala ranchlands, cattle country with a crisp, cool climate and velvety smooth hills.

FAR RIGHT: Snowcapped Mauna Kea is the world's largest mountain, if you count the thousands of feet between the ocean floor and sea level.

BELOW: Waipio Valley is a remote area at the end of Highway 24 that is still used for taro farming.

OPPOSITE PAGE: Puako Petroglyphs near Waikoloa, one of the largest petroglyph fields in the islands, are carved on pahoehoe lava.

Photographed by Douglas Peebles
Written by Sam Malvaney
Produced by Bennett Hymer

Title type: Trooper Roman
Headline type: Berling
Text type: Eras Book
Caption type: Eras Medium
Typesetting by: Unitype, Inc.

Printed and bound in Korea

INDEX: DESCRIPTION OF SITES AND SIGHTS

OAHU

housed Hawaii's government—the House of Representatives met in the throne room, the Senate in the royal dining room—until 1969, when the new state capitol nearby was completed. Iolani means "the hawk of heaven," a symbol to Hawaiians of highest royalty.

KAENA POINT p. 27

Some of the largest coastal waves in the world—sometimes reaching 40 to 50 feet—crash off Kaena Point. The westernmost point of Oahu, Kaena Point was once the site for a fishing village, several *heiau* and some fishing shrines. The demigod Maui once attempted, unsuccessfully as it turns out, to join together Kauai and Oahu from here. The point was also believed to be the main spot on Oahu where souls of the dying were taken from earth by the gods. Kaena was the name of a brother of Pele, the fire goddess.

KAILUA BEACH PARK p. 21

Oahu's prime windsurfing spot, Kailua Beach Park is located on windward Oahu at the eastern end of Kailua Bay. This thirty-acre park is popular with locals and visitors alike. Offshore from the beach is flat Popoi'a Island, which means "rotten fish," probably a reference to an old fishing shrine and its offerings located on the island. Unfortunately, the shrine was wiped out by a tidal wave in 1946.

KANEOHE BAY p. 6

Kaneohe Bay and the surrounding area lies within the boundary of an old volcano caldera. The bay is protected by a three-mile-long barrier reef, the only major barrier reef in the main Hawaiian islands. The bay and its shoreline were the sites of intensive aquaculture by the early Hawaiians, and by the time European contact was made with Hawaii, Kaneohe Bay had probably the largest aquaculture industry in the islands. Some of the fish ponds remain today.

KAPIOLANI PARK— NATATORIUM p. 13

Kapiolani Park, named for the wife of King Kalakaua, was Hawaii's first public park, dedicated on Kamehameha Day, June 11, 1877. Within this 100-acre park near Diamond Head are a bandstand, the Waikiki Shell amphitheater, Honolulu Zoo, Waikiki Aquarium, the famous Kodak Hula Show and acres of open land. It is also the finish for the world-class Honolulu Marathon. On the ocean side of Kapiolani Park is the Waikiki War Memorial Natatorium, built in 1927 for swimming. It has since fallen into disuse and decay.

KAWAIAHAO CHURCH p. 37

The church was finished in 1842, twenty-two years after the land underneath was assigned by the monarch to the first Congregationalist missionaries. It took five years to build the church from 14,000 coral blocks cut from ocean reefs. Kawaiahao means "fresh water pool of Hao," who was a chiefess, and is named after an ancient spring. Services are performed in both English and Hawaiian.

KING KAMEHAMEHA STATUE p. 36

This statue—unveiled at King Kalakaua's 1883 coronation—is actually a replica of a commissioned statue lost when the ship carrying it from Europe sank off the Falkland Islands. The original, however, was later retrieved and brought to Hawaii, where it now stands in the town of Kohala on the Big Island, closer to the birthplace of Kamehameha the Great. The sculptor used photographs of a Honolulu businessman to sculpt the statue, and thus it bears little actual resemblance to Kamehameha. The barbed *pololu*, or spear, in his left hand symbolizes peace; the right arm is extended in *aloha*.

LANIKAI BEACH p. 39

Lanikai Beach fronts one of Oahu's earlier residential developments. Promoters gave the community the name Lanikai, which has no meaning in Hawaiian. Located between Kailua Bay and Waimanalo Bay, the mile-long beach is popular with locals for its calm waters. The area was once an ancient fishing site and, later, the site of several watermelon plantations. Two offshore islands and landmarks called the Mokuluas are protected bird sanctuaries.

MISSION HOUSES p. 38

The main house, built in 1821, can be considered a prefabricated building. New England wood was first cut and fitted in Boston before making the trip around Cape Horn to Hawaii. The houses are the oldest remaining Western-style buildings in Hawaii, and are now operated as a museum.

MT. OLOMANA/KAILUA p. 18

The peak of Olomana, on windward Oahu, is within an ancient volcanic caldera that also contains the towns of Kaneohe and Kailua. The primal-looking peaks are the remains of erosion-resistant lava dikes near the caldera's southern rim.

NUUANU PALI p. 19

Gale-force winds often make this overlook one of the windiest spots on Oahu. Nuuanu means "the cool height" and early mornings atop this thousand-foot-high overlook are

BIG ISLAND

AHUENA HEIAU p. 101
This reconstructed *heiau* was once covered by a hotel that was later demolished. The owners of the new King Kamehameha Hotel, built further back from the *heiau* site, restored the *heiau* under the direction of the Bishop Museum. In his old age, Kamehameha the Great made this spot—called Kamakahonu, eye of the turtle—home from where he ruled his newly-united Hawaiian kingdom. In 1819, he died here; his bones were hidden in a place so secret that they have never been found.

CITY OF REFUGE pp. 99, 100
Commonly called the City of Refuge, this national historical park is properly called Pu'uhonua o Honaunau. When an ancient Hawaiian broke a sacred law—a *kapu*— or was fleeing the enemy in war, this *pu'uhonua* could offer a safe haven, if they could get to it. Once inside, the person was absolved by a *kahuna*, or priest. Covering six acres, Pu'uhonua o Honaunau contains a number of structures, including the 1,000-foot-long Great Wall, ten feet high and seventeen feet wide, constructed without mortar from lava rock in the mid-1550s.

HAPUNA BEACH PARK p. 107
White sand beaches are scarce on the Big Island, and Hapuna Beach is probably the island's best. Half a mile long, the beach can reach 200 feet in width during summer. The adjacent state park provides shelters, restrooms, showers and large grassy areas. In addition to the excellent beach itself, its facilities, sunny weather (less than ten inches of rain a year) and the diversity of activities make Hapuna Beach the Big Island's most popular recreational area.

HULIHEE PALACE p. 105
Filled with furnishings and objects from the 19th century, the Hulihee Palace was built in 1838 by Big Island governor John Adams Kuakini. This royal edifice—King Kalakaua favored it as a summer retreat—is a two-story building of coral and lava.

KAIMU BEACH, KALAPANA p. 94
This black sand beach was formed in the mid-1700s when hot lava from Kilauea reached the ocean; steam explosions pulverized the lava into sand. Black sand beaches appear and disappear regularly, and Kaimu Beach is slowly disappearing into the ocean. A 1975 earthquake dropped the beach and ocean floor three feet, further diminishing the beach. New black sand beaches are being formed near Kalapana, down the coast from Kaimu Beach, as Kilauea continues sending lava into the sea.

KILAUEA CALDERA pp. 96–97

KILAUEA VOLCANO pp. 91, 95
Although Kilauea shot a geyser of lava a record 1,900 feet into the air in 1950, compared with the more violent volcanoes along the Pacific Rim or in the Mediterranean, Hawaii's volcanoes are generally low-key and safely witnessed by visitors during eruptions.

A typical eruption of Kilauea begins when there is a change of pressure in the underground molten rock. Seeking the path of least resistance, lava will surge upward through a crack or rift in the caldera. Released lava either forms a lake of molten lava above previously-cooled lava in the caldera, or it flows down slopes of the volcano. Kilauea is the current home of Pele, goddess of fire, who is responsible for volcanoes and earthquakes. Over the years, legends say that she has moved from Kauai, to Oahu, to Maui and finally to the Big Island; geological evidence substantiates her wanderings in the islands.

KING KAMEHAMEHA STATUE p. 108

KOHALA pp. 108–109
A mixed landscape of dry desert and lush mountains, the district of Kohala is rich with legends and history. Ancient archaeological sites are among the best in the Hawaiian islands. A number of *heiau* and village sites are found in this part of the Big Island, including the family *heiau* of Kamehameha I. In the 1880s, sugar cane dominated north Kohala; a narrow-gauge railroad was built from the northern tip of the island to the port of Mahukona.

KONA pp. 102–103, 104–105
The fastest-growing spot in Hawaii during the 1980s, the Kona coast has some of Hawaii's driest land and sunniest weather. Coffee and macadamia nut plantations sit on lava flows from the late 1800s; ancient petroglyphs

carved into old *pahoehoe* lava from earlier flows are found in Kona. Captain Cook lost his life on the Kona coast.

LILIUOKALANI GARDENS p. 90

This thirty-acre park in Hilo is named after Queen Liliuokalani, Hawaii's only female monarch. The sister of King Kalakaua, her royal reign lasted just two years before Honolulu businessmen and American marines overthrew her monarchy, Hawaii's last. Located near the hotel district on Banyan Drive, Liliuokalani Gardens is a Japanese garden of stone lanterns and bridges, a tea ceremony house, footpaths, pagodas and pools.

MAUNA KEA p. 109

Classified as volcanically dormant, Mauna Kea rises to 13,796 feet, guaranteed to capture snow even in tropical latitudes. Indeed, Mauna Kea means "white mountain." In the last ice age, glaciers slithered down the slopes; glacial moraines and permafrost beneath the rocky crust remain today. Astronomers from Canada, France, England and the United States have erected reflecting telescopes atop Mauna Kea, whose altitude and remoteness assures crystalline viewing of the stars. For centuries, before European intrusions, the early Hawaiians found high-grade basalt for stone tools in a summit quarry.

MAUNA LOA p. 106

The most massive single mountain—and active volcano—on earth, Mauna Loa has an estimated volume of 10,000 cubic miles. It is named for its shape: long or broad mountain. Mauna Loa is 119 feet lower than its island companion, Mauna Kea. (Both mountains are higher than Mount Everest, if measured from

their true bases on the sea's floor.) Mauna Loa has sent lava down its slopes often in historical times. Hilo, the island's largest city that was built on lava flows only a few centuries old, has been threatened several times. For three decades, the Mauna Loa Weather Observatory at 11,200 feet on the northern slope has sampled the atmosphere. Among the results: air this far out in the middle of nowhere shows increasing carbon dioxide levels, supporting proponents of the green house theory.

PUAKO PETROGLYPHS p. 111

PUUKOHOLA HEIAU p. 98

Overlooking Kawaihae Bay, Puukohola Heiau—originally built in the mid-1550s— was rebuilt by Kamehameha I for the war god Kukailimoku. His chief military rival was invited to its dedication in 1791; Kamehameha had him killed as a sacrifice at the *heiau*. Nineteen years after the dedication, Kamehameha had unified all the islands into the Kingdom of Hawaii. The largest restored *heiau* in Hawaii and now a national historic site, the *heiau* measures 224 feet by 100 feet.

RAINBOW FALLS p. 92

Rainbow Falls, only a few minutes away from downtown Hilo, is a cascading waterfall eighty feet in height, with an average discharge of 303.5 million gallons of water every day.

ST. PETER'S CHURCH p. 103

WAILUA FALLS p. 93

WAIPIO VALLEY p. 110

This broad and deep valley is fed by a river with twin waterfalls. An important wetland location, the valley was once home to

Hawaiian farmers who tended garden terraces and irrigated patches of taro. It was also an important political and cultural center before the arrival of Captain Cook. The valley was also an important ancient aquaculture site, with freshwater ponds of fish. Two tidal waves flooded the valley after World War II. The Peace Corps trained volunteers here in the 1960s for duty in rural Asia. Large flocks of bats on feeding flights can be seen at dusk in the valley.

WAILEA p. 50

Wailea is one of five beaches in the Wailea resort area. Formerly called Kahamanini, this beach and the others along the two-mile stretch of shoreline came to be known as Wailea when the coastal lands were purchased by the Matson Navigation Company. Later, in the 1970s, when the area was developed, the resort retained the name Wailea. Wailea means "the water of Lea," who was the goddess of canoe makers.

WAILUA FALLS p. 57

WEST MAUI MOUNTAINS p. 51, 61

Maui consists of two fused volcanic peaks; Haleakala and West Maui. The older of the two volcanoes by hundreds of thousands of years, West Maui's summit of Puu Kukui, 5,788 feet above sea level, is Hawaii's second rainiest spot. There is geological evidence on West Maui of a shoreline about 250 feet above the present sea level; it is thought to be the highest level of the sea in Hawaii from a global ice melt during the Pleistocene epoch. Lava from the younger volcano of Haleakala flowed to the slopes of the West Maui volcano, forming a land bridge that is now the agricultural valley between West Maui and Haleakala.

MOLOKAI

KALAUPAPA pp. 62, 64

A Catholic Belgian priest, Father Damien, arrived on the Kalaupapa Peninsula in 1873, where he stayed until his death sixteen years later. Kalaupapa was a colony for lepers, and in his sixteen years, Father Damien turned the leper colony into a unified community. The peninsula was designated a national historic monument in 1975, and is now administered by the National Park Service.

ST. PHILOMENA CHURCH p. 63

The church was but a small and simple structure when Father Damien arrived in Kalaupapa in 1873. A pandanus tree next to the church was Damien's shelter for several weeks after his arrival. Over the next couple of decades, Damien and others enlarged the church. When he died, Damien was buried next to the tree, which no longer exists. A stucco finish was applied to the church's concrete facing in the 1940s.

WAILUA BEACH/VALLEY p. 66

KAUAI

ALAKOKO FISHPOND p. 81

A stone wall isolates an elbow in the Huleia River, creating a large pond used by the early Hawaiians for raising fish. While the ancient Hawaiians often built aquaculture ponds in coastal areas, this inland pond is exceptional in its size and in the craftsmanship of the 900-foot-long stone wall. Legend says the Menehune people, who worked on a project only after dark and only for one night, were commissioned by a princess and her brother to build the pond. The Menehune told the siblings that they could not watch. But they did, and the couple turned to stone.

FERN GROTTO pp. 72–73

HANALEI pp. 70, 86

While it is one of Kauai's wettest spots, the island's north shore is considered by many to be Hawaii's most exquisite retreat. The nearly-perfect crescent of Hanalei Bay is the largest bay on Kauai. (Hanalei means "crescent bay.") In the summer, when the water is smooth, the bay is used as an anchorage by yachts from around the world. In winter, when storms to the north whip up twenty- to thirty-foot waves, it is a surfer's dream.

HANALEI VALLEY pp. 71, 84–85, 86

By the middle 1800s, Hanalei Valley was a center of coffee-growing in the Hawaiian Islands. Other introduced crops—peaches, pineapples, sugar cane, oranges, bananas, and rice—competed for attention with the taro fields of the native population. There were also efforts at silk production using mulberry trees and silkworms from China. Taro has returned as a major crop in the valley, which is now also a designated wildlife preserve. The one-lane bridge across the river prevents tour buses from entering the valley.

HANAPEPE SALT FLATS pp. 76–77

Early Hawaiians on both Kauai and the island of Niihau (on the horizon in the photograph) developed a trade in salt. Seawater was allowed to evaporate in the salt ponds. A crust of dried salt was left, which was collected. A local group called Hui Hana Pa'akai 'O Hanapepe still collects salt from the Hanapepe salt ponds, but because it does not meet government standards for purity (it is often somewhat red from clay residue), it cannot be commercially sold. Nonetheless, many locals prefer this salt.

KALALAU BEACH p. 81

KALALAU VALLEY p. 80

Kalalau Valley is at the end of an eleven-mile trail that begins at Haena Beach Park, near Hanalei. At the bottom of the valley is Kalalau Beach, which has a waterfall at one end and a stream at the other. Kalalau Valley is the largest valley along the Na Pali Coast. For centuries, Hawaiians lived in many valleys along the Na Pali Coast, and in Kalalau Valley are the remains of stone-lined taro patches and home sites, some used until early in this century by native Hawaiians.

KILAUEA LIGHTHOUSE p. 82

Built in 1913, the 52-foot-high Kilauea Lighthouse claims the largest clamshell lens in the world. When it was operating, it sent out a flash—visible up to twenty miles out at sea—every ten seconds. The effort of rotation was considerable: the light's moving parts weighed four tons. An automated beacon replaced the lighthouse in 1967. Located in the Kilauea Point National Wildlife Refuge, the promontory is a nesting site for red-footed boobies and wedge-tailed shearwaters.

KOKEE STATE PARK p. 80

Kalalau Valley offers a beautiful view from the heights of Kokee State Park. Normally reached by a hiking trail along the Na Pali Coast, Kalalau Valley was once accessible from the uplands of Kokee State Park. While Kokee is the only populated place in Kauai's uplands, it is also an important wildlife and plant preserve. Within the park, one can rent state-owned cabins. The Kokee Lodge offers a restaurant and other visitor amenities, and next door is the Kokee Museum with its

natural history exhibits. Near this state park is Manhattan-size Alakai Swamp.

LUMAHAI BEACH pp. 86–87

MT. WAIALEALE p. 81

While rainfall over the open ocean near Kauai typically averages twenty-five to thirty inches yearly, Mt. Waialeale (5,148 feet above sea level) captures and releases moisture in the trade winds as they collide with the mountain. The result is the world's wettest and rainiest spot. The ability to capture rain is characteristic of Hawaii's taller islands, where rainfall patterns imitate topographical contours. Small islands in a larger island's rain shadow—Niihau lies in Kauai's rain shadow, for example—are considerably drier and without lush vegetation.

NA PALI pp. 87, 88

A highway nearly encircles Kauai, save for the thirteen rugged miles of the Na Pali coastline. No roads enter Na Pali Coast, only a single hiking trail eleven miles long—built by ancient Hawaiians—from Haena to Kalalau Beach. On the western edge of Na Pali is Polihale Beach Park; to the east, Haena Beach Park.

PRINCEVILLE p. 82

A hotel, thirty-six holes of golf and 1,200 condominiums cover this 1,000-acre resort, once an expanse of pastureland. When Queen Emma and King Kamehameha IV visited Hanalei in 1860, their two-year-old son, Prince Albert Edward Kauikeaouli Leiopapa a Kamehameha, so charmed the owner of the land that he named it Princeville. Unfortunately, the young prince died two years later. A Russian gun emplacement—Fort Alexander—was once perched atop the cliffs.

SPOUTING HORN BLOWHOLE p. 75

Where lava flows have reached the ocean, one will inevitably find a blowhole like Spouting Horn. As lava makes its way to the coast, it sometimes will cool and harden over material that is softer than the cooled lava. Wave action then erodes this softer layer to create a hole from which water gushes. Moaning sounds, attributed in legends to mythological lizard creatures stuck in the hole, are in fact caused by suction from the wave action.

TREE TUNNEL p. 74

WAILUA FALLS p. 73

WAILUA RIVER p. 72

Wailua means twin waters, and up the river one will find, given enough rain, two water-falls cascading over an eighty-foot cliff. It is said that Hawaiian chiefs would show their courage by diving into the river here. Along the Wailua River are ancient *heiau* and other remnants of the past, like Pohaku-ho'o-hanau, the royal birthing stone. Persons of high rank were born here and their umbilical cords wrapped and hidden within the cracks of the stone.

WAIMEA CANYON pp. 71, 78–79

Waimea Canyon, some twelve miles long and 3,657 feet at its deepest, is slowly being washed out to sea by the Waimea River. Long ago, a giant summit caldera some ten to twelve miles across capped Kauai's volcano. Kauai's flat uplands resulted from the ancient horizontal lava beds once located deep inside the caldera. Waimea Canyon slices into this old caldera, and today it continues to erode further back into the caldera's remains. The headwaters of the Waimea River are in the nearby Alakai Swamp.

indeed chilly. One of the few passes over the Koolau Mountains between windward Oahu and Honolulu, Nuuanu Pali was the culmination of the Battle of Nuuanu Valley in 1795. Following his battle successes on Maui, Lanai and Molokai, Kamehameha the Great landed his war canoes at Waikiki and forced Oahu's armies up to Nuuanu Pali and defeat.

PEARL HARBOR pp. 28–29
A reef barrier at its entrance once made Pearl Harbor inaccessible to Western sailing ships. In 1884, the Hawaiian government allowed the United States to dredge the harbor and establish a naval station within Pearl Harbor. Little work on the station was done, however, until annexation of the Hawaiian Islands by the United States in 1898. Pearl Harbor took its name from a river—Waimomi, meaning water of the pearl—that emptied into the harbor. Long ago, pearl oysters were abundant in Pearl Harbor, but pollution destroyed the original oyster beds.

POLYNESIAN CULTURAL CENTER p. 22
One of the longest-running and most consistently sold-out shows in the United States, the Polynesian Cultural Center is located in the northern Oahu town of Laie. Owned by the Mormon Church (most of Laie's population is Mormon), the Center opened in 1964. Authentic villages and performances by Mormon students from Pacific islands depict early cultures from Hawaii, Fiji, Samoa, the Marquesas, Tahiti and New Zealand.

PUNCHBOWL CRATER p. 36–37
The Hawaiian name for this extinct volcano was Puowaina, or hill of sacrifice. Indeed, human sacrifices were offered here centuries ago. Today, the 114-acre crater bottom is a cemetery for 26,000 dead from World Wars I and II, the Korean War and the Vietnam War.

RABBIT ISLAND p. 21
The island's proper name is Manana, but it once was used as a rabbit farm by a local plantation owner and so the name Rabbit Island became more common. In 1932, Rabbit Island was considered for a prison camp. The island, an old volcanic crater, is a state-protected seabird sanctuary.

WAIKIKI pp. 8, 9, 10–11, 14, 15
Once a swamp fed by mountain streams and springwaters, Waikiki, which means "spouting water," and its beach—with its coconut groves, fine surf and good fishing—was a popular resort for early Hawaiians. The best surfing waves were reserved for royalty. In the 1860s, the first dirt road was opened between Waikiki and the growing city of Honolulu. In 1884, the first resort opened at Sans Souci near Diamond Head, and in 1901, Waikiki's first real hotel, the Moana, opened on the beach.

WAIMEA BAY pp. 24–25
In winter, when northern storms off Alaska churn up the Pacific, Waimea Bay has the largest surfing waves in the world. During the rest of the year, the waters here are usually placid and flat. At any time of the year, a spectacular view of Waimea Bay is found from Puu o Mahuka Heiau, located on the plateau behind the bay and one of the largest *heiau* on Oahu. Contact between foreigners and Hawaiians on Oahu first occurred at Waimea, when the ships of Captain Cook—he had just been killed on the Big Island—landed at Waimea for water.

MAUI

FLEMING BEACH p. 41
Locals still call it Fleming Beach, but since the mid-1970s, when the shoreline around the beach was developed into a resort, it has been called Kapalua Beach, which means "two borders." David T. Fleming, an early manager with Honolua Ranch and Baldwin Packers, developed the coast of Kapalua Beach into a public park.

HALEAKALA pp. 52, 53
Of the sunrise from Haleakala's summit, Mark Twain wrote, "It was the sublimest spectacle I ever witnessed, and I think the memory of it will remain with me always." Thousands of visitors drive each year to the 10,023-foot summit—which geologists believe was originally 3,000 feet higher—in predawn hours to witness the sunrise. The crater—twenty-one miles in circumference, 3,000 feet deep and nineteen square miles—is not really of volcanic origin. It was formed when two valleys, formed by a million years of erosion, eventually joined at the summit. Eruptions covered the joined valley floors with great cinder cones and lava. Haleakala last erupted in 1790.

HAMOA BEACH p. 56

While the actual origin of the name "Hamoa" is not certain, some believe it is a shortened version of Ha'amoa, which is an old name for Samoa. Unprotected from the open sea, the surf off this 1,000-foot-long beach was a favorite surfing spot in ancient times, as it is today. Access to the beach is on private property owned by the Hana Ranch Company, owner of the Hotel Hana Maui. The beach has been used by the Hotel Hana Maui since the 1930s.

HANA pp. 58–59, 60

The road to Hana is the most famous road in the islands with its 673 curves and sixty bridges. During the 1800s, this fertile region tempted many entrepreneurs to grow sugar cane, cotton, pineapple, eucalyptus, vanilla and even rubber. Indeed, Hana had the first rubber-producing plantation in America. In earlier days, Hana offered Kamehameha the Great many problems. Although the rest of Maui had fallen to the Big Island armies of Kamehameha, opposition in Hana stopped Kamehameha's complete conquest of Maui for several years. At one time during the battle, is said that more than a thousand war canoes from the Big Island filled Hana Bay.

HOOKIPA pp. 54–55

Hookipa is world-famous for its windsurfing, and to a lesser degree, its board surfing, which began locally here in the 1930s. Once a wide sandy beach, a tidal wave in 1946 reduced much of the beach to a small sand strip faced with a rocky shelf. Swimming here is not safe because of the rock shelf and ocean currents. Hookipa means "hospitality."

IAO NEEDLE pp. 42–43

This vertical pinnacle is nestled within West Maui's ancient and dormant volcanic crater. The 2,250-foot cinder cone remnant is a popular site. Nearby, in 1790, Kamehameha the Great was assured of his Maui conquest when he defeated his enemies in a vicious battle; he was assisted by two Englishmen, John Young and Isaac Davis. The battle left the Iao Stream red with blood and bodies.

JODO BUDDHIST MISSION p. 42

This site commemorates the first Japanese immigrants to Hawaii, and in 1968, this Buddha—the largest Buddha outside of Asia—was dedicated for the centennial of their arrival.

KAANAPALI pp. 46, 47

Three decades ago, Kaanapali was mostly fields of sugar cane. In the early 1960s, Amfac Corporation developed a large section of agricultural land along the three-mile beach into Hawaii's first megaresort. The geological focus of Kaanapali is Black Rock, a volcanic cinder cone. Hawaiian tradition says that Black Rock, or Pu'u Keka'a, was a "soul's leap." As a person was nearing death, the soul rambled over the island. If commitments in this world had been met, the soul ended up at Pu'u Keka'a, to be taken by the gods. At that precise time, physical death would occur.

KAPALUA p. 48

Located on Maui's northwest coast, Kapalua has two eighteen-hole golf courses, 194 hotel rooms and 180 villas. Once a pineapple plantation, this 750-acre resort includes the site of a massive burial ground for ancient Hawaiians.

LAHAINA pp. 40, 43, 44–45

Long before it became a whaling town, Lahaina was a popular retreat with Hawaiian royalty. After his victory in Iao Valley, Kamehameha the Great set up a residence in Lahaina. His son, Kamehameha II, named Lahaina the kingdom's capital, and it remained the governmental center of Hawaii until 1845. Despite its open anchorage, whaling ships anchored at Lahaina in between cruises for sperm whales. But Lahaina soon yielded to Honolulu, which increased in political and economic importance. Herman Melville, author of *Moby Dick*, visited Lahaina in 1843, but unable to find a suitable job, he went to Honolulu.

MOLOKINI p. 49

Located mid-way between Maui and Kaho'olawe, the ancient crater rim rises about 150 feet above clear waters. There are no beaches on Molokini, but the waters are a popular snorkeling and diving spot. In 1977, the Molokini Shoal Marine Life Conservation District was established to protect the waters off Molokini. Legend has it that the island was once a beautiful woman who was turned into stone by Pele, the fire goddess.

SEVEN POOLS pp. 56–57

Part of Haleakala National Park, these plunge pools are formed along the Ohe'o Stream in a deep gulch. While the pools themselves are popular swimming holes, powerful currents and frequent sharks make the ocean at the stream's mouth unsafe for swimming. Next to the pools are the stone remains of an ancient Hawaiian village. Somewhere along the way, the pools got the erroneous name of Seven *Sacred* Pools; in fact, the early Hawaiians did not consider them sacred.